CREEPY
CASTLES

BY
Christine Sotnak Rom

Illustrated
by
David Rickman

CRESTWOOD HOUSE
New York

J 133.1
ROM

Library of Congress Cataloging-in-Publication Data
Rom, Christine Sotnak.
 Creepy castles / by Christine Sotnak Rom.

  p.   cm. — (Incredible histories)
 Includes bibliographical references.
 SUMMARY: Describes the ghosts that haunt various European castles.
 ISBN 0-89686-505-3
 1. Ghosts—Europe—Juvenile literature. 2. Castles—Europe—Miscellanea—Juvenile literature. [1. Ghosts—
Europe. 2. Castles—Europe—Miscellanea.] 1. Title. 11. Series.
 BF1472.E85R66 1990   133.1'22—dc20   89-28986
                                                                                        CIP
                                                                                        AC

Illustration Credits
Cover: Kristi Schaeppi
Interior: David Rickman

Copyright © 1990 by Crestwood House, Macmillan Publishing Company

All rights reserved. No part of this book may be reproduced or transmitted in any form or by any means, electronic
or mechanical, including photocopying, recording, or by any information storage and retrieval system, without
permission in writing from the Publisher.

Macmillan Publishing Company
866 Third Avenue
New York, NY 10022
Collier Macmillan Canada, Inc.

CRESTWOOD HOUSE

Printed in the United States of America

First Edition

10 9 8 7 6 5 4 3 2 1

10.95

Contents

∧∧∧∧∧∧∧∧∧∧∧∧∧∧∧∧∧∧∧∧∧∧∧∧

903466

Introduction

During the Middle Ages, castles were the homes of people who ruled their lands. The word *castle* comes from the Latin word *castrum*, meaning fort. In Old English, *castle* means hill fort or walled town. From the safe castle fortress, the ruler governed the people and the land around the castle. He even had his own armies to protect himself and his people.

The castle was the center of medieval life. It has been said that much of Europe's history can be found within castle walls.

Every castle was different.Some were built to be lived in and were beautiful. Others were used for defense and were dark and sinister. Each castle was shaped by the lives and personalities of the people who lived there.

Often castles were named after the families who built them. Each family passed the castle on to children or relatives. The castle stayed with the family until it was either captured or, in modern times, sold.

The atmosphere inside the castle was determined by the master who built and commanded it. He could make the castle a place of strength and safety, or it could be a place of fear and death. Many rulers were cruel. Often servants' lives depended on how well they pleased their rulers.

The constant struggle between life and death at the time had a powerful impact on people's memories. The drama of real events was often mixed with imagination to weave great stories about these mighty homes and their rulers.

People's fear of the unknown makes death mysterious and frightening. Mystery cries out for explanation. For some, the idea of ghosts can be a comforting link to life after death.

Many stories about castle ghosts come from people's memories of sad events. The ghosts in these stories and legends are called historic ghosts. They seem to be trapped in time and act as reminders of events. They usually are seen at the places where they lived.

Other ghosts reported in castles are spirits who appear with messages for the living. Still others haunt a person or a place without a known reason. Some of these haunting spirits may appear only once, while others stay around for hundreds of years.

Some castles claim to have poltergeists. *Poltergeist* is the German word for noisy ghost. These noisy ghosts make all kinds of strange sounds that no one can explain. Some people say things have been thrown at them or they have been touched or shoved by an unseen hand. There have been reports of poltergeists for more than 1,500 years from all parts of the world. Some researchers think poltergeists are living people who use some unknown power of their minds or spirits.

A lot of people don't believe in ghosts. They think people who see ghosts are seeing things they want to see. Some think these people's minds are playing tricks on them.

Other people think "ghosts" are caused by some natural effect like wind, sunlight, or changes in the atmosphere.

There are many ideas about who or what ghosts really are. There are also hundreds of castles that are reported to be haunted.

The castles in this book are some of the most famous haunted places in Great Britain and France. Many people who have been in these castles have ghost stories to tell. Some of these stories are recorded in written history. Other accounts are recent and mysterious.

Are the castles really haunted? Or are the strange events caused by something unknown? No matter how people answer these questions, everyone will probably agree that these are very creepy castles.

Glamis Castle

Every great Scots family, especially in the Highlands, had its own storyteller who kept track of the family's history. During the 13th century, important information was recorded in stories about the family's births, marriages, and deaths. The Scottish Highlanders from powerful families had their storytellers record feuds and clan battles. The storytellers also told of the family's ghosts. It is from legends such as these that Glamis Castle became known as one of the most haunted castles on earth.

Glamis Castle was built in the 13th century. Sir John Lyon was the first of the great Lyon family to live at Glamis Castle. He was tall and fair and was nicknamed the White Lyon. He married Princess Joanna, daughter of King Robert II of Scotland.

Sir John Lyon was king of his castle. As king, he had the power over life and death. He and the kings of Glamis who followed him had their own army for more than 600 years. Later members of the Lyon family also hired their own hangman because the early kings of Glamis Castle were the judges of law and order. This power was ordained by the royal Scottish kings. It is said that the Lyons never abused their power. Even so, the Hangman's Chamber is one room at Glamis that no one will sleep in.

The Lyon family has owned Glamis Castle for over 600 years. It has more ghosts and terrible tales attached to it than any other castle of its kind.

Glamis Castle was built with pointed turrets and dark battlements. It was built as a family stronghold in the Scottish baronial style. This style was popular with wealthy land owners who wanted a grand-looking residence. The castle was designed for style and appearance rather than to serve as a military fortress. With its fairy-tale-like appearance and its gray-pink stones, it looks like the perfect place for a ghost.

In his play *Macbeth*, the famous playwright William Shakespeare mentioned Glamis as the place King Duncan was murdered. Visitors who are shown the murder room often report a sinister feeling.

Another room at Glamis Castle has a bloodstain on the floor that will not come off. King Malcolm was said to have been murdered in that room. The stain is in the outline of a body. Since no guest or servant would stay there, the room was walled up. Actually, King Malcolm was murdered in the 11th century, before Glamis Castle was built, but the legend continues.

High in an abandoned tower there is a room where Alexander Crawford, the fourth earl of Crawford, quarreled with one lord of Glamis and two Scottish chieftains. The earl was visiting from Finavon Castle. One legend claims that Lord Crawford was a drinking companion who often caused trouble at Glamis Castle. Because of his magnificent beard, he was given the name Earl Beardie. He was said to have such a bad reputation that he was nicknamed the "Wicked Earl."

Earl Beardie drank a lot and played cards on Sunday. He liked to gamble so much that when no one would play cards with him on Sunday, he would grow very angry. During a famous quarrel, he finally shouted that he would play with the devil himself. Suddenly, there was a knock on the castle door. In walked a stranger who challenged him to a game. It is said that Earl Beardie lost his soul gambling with the devil, and his spirit is doomed to play cards or dice until Judgment Day.

A castle cook has heard the sound of dice and loud stamping and cursing coming from the tower late at night. Some say Earl Beardie's ghost roams the castle looking for someone to play cards with. A chamber called the Blue Room is also said to be haunted by the ghost of Earl Beardie. His ghost is most often heard on stormy nights in November.

There is a vampire legend at Glamis Castle as well. One servant woman was supposedly caught sucking the blood from one of her victims. As punishment, she was walled up in a room. Vampires, however, can't die unless a stake is driven through their hearts, so she lives on behind the wall. Some people think the wall is in danger of crumbling. If it does, the vampire will be released.

Some of these legends were made up for fun by writers. Other stories have been changed to make them more dramatic. A few of the stories seem to be partly true, though, or even entirely true.

The legend of the monster of Glamis could be partly true, for example. The monster, who was half man, half beast, was said to be kept secretly in a locked room. In reality, the "monster" was probably the deformed son of an early earl of Strathmore.

In 1821, the first son of the eleventh earl of Strathmore was born. But he did not look human and was reported to have died at birth. Legend says, however, that he did not die but grew to be very strong.

He was locked up in a secret room, built to hide him from the world. Only the people in charge of the castle knew he was there. Since the monster was the true heir to the estate of Glamis, each earl in line to inherit the estate had to learn the secret of the locked room. When each earl became 21 years of age, he was shown the secret.

One lady of Strathmore is said to have asked to know the secret. She was told, "If you could only guess the nature of the secret, you would go down on your knees and thank God it was not yours."

In 1880, a Scottish newspaper ran a story about a workman at Glamis Castle. While making some repairs, he accidentally knocked a hole in a wall. He found a secret passageway with a locked door at the end. He became frightened and reported it to the castle steward. The steward looked after the castle's affairs. Not long after that, the workman disappeared. It was thought that the steward paid the workman a lot of money to go to another country and keep the secret to himself.

Some say the earls of Strathmore spread rumors about ghosts. They hoped to keep attention away from the real secret.

The present Lord Strathmore doesn't know about a monster. The deformed earl was probably dead when this Lord Strathmore inherited the castle. Some think he lived to be incredibly old and only died in 1941. Lord Strathmore thinks there was a coffin bricked up behind one of the castle walls.

Many more ghosts are said to haunt Glamis Castle. One is the ghost of a gray lady that appeared to the Dowager Countess Granville. One sunny day the countess walked into the chapel. There, kneeling in one of the pews, outlined in sunlight, was a pale figure saying her prayers. Lord Strathmore walked into the chapel and saw the very same image. Later he saw the gray lady walk into the chapel.

A small dressing room used to be haunted, too. Often, people who slept there felt the sheets being pulled off the bed. Nothing has happened since it became a bathroom, however.

Also at Glamis is a room where a door opens by itself every night. It has even opened after being bolted and wedged by a heavy object.

A ghost of a woman runs across the castle park. She points to her bloody mouth, open and tongueless. She is probably the ghost of a poor woman who had her tongue cut out as punishment.

A strange, thin ghost called "Jack the Runner" is sometimes seen running wildly up the castle driveway.

A madman is said to walk along part of the roof on stormy nights. This area is known as the Mad Earl's Walk. The deformed earl may have tried to escape here. It could also be the place where he got his exercise.

There is a ghost of a small black servant who was treated unkindly more than 200 years ago. He has been seen in the sitting room of the Queen Mother, Lady Elizabeth Bowes-Lyon.

The white lady of the clock tower is thought to be the ghost of Janet Douglas. She was the wife of the sixth Lord Glamis and was accused of trying to poison King James V. She was also accused of being a witch. She was burned for her crimes in 1537 at Castle Hill in Edinburgh, even though there was no evidence of her guilt. Her hovering figure is often seen surrounded by a red, fiery glow. Others say she was walled up alive in the castle. Her spirit is said to haunt her prison room. Another story claims that, because of her powers of witchcraft, she is still alive after 400 years.

There is no question that Glamis Castle has many mysteries. Perhaps the strangest of all is the mystery of the secret rooms. One party of young people tried to find the secret rooms. They went to every room in the castle and hung towels and sheets out of every window. These were to serve as markers. When they went outside to make sure all of the windows were marked, they counted seven windows with nothing there.

What is in those rooms? Where are the doors that lead to them? There are no answers to these questions. They are still mysteries.

Hermitage Castle

Hermitage Castle was a massive fortress. It was built in the 13th century on the border between England and Scotland in Roxburghshire, Scotland. The road leading to the castle is wild and very lonely.

Since England and Scotland were always at war, this border castle was continually changing hands. To each captured owner, that usually meant a gruesome death.

The lords of the castle often threw their enemies into the dungeon and left them there to die. One of these unfortunate men was Alexander Ramsay, the sheriff of Teviotdale. He was thrown into the dungeon to starve, and people say his ghost has not found rest.

The ghost of Mary, Queen of Scots is said to visit Hermitage Castle. She once rode 50 miles alone across the wild moors. Her mission was to comfort her lover, the earl of Bothwell. The Bothwells were then the owners of Hermitage Castle. The earl had been badly wounded and lay in great pain. Mary caught a fever from her ride that day and almost died. Since this was a place that had been important during their lives, both of the lovers' ghosts have been reported to haunt the Hermitage.

Other ghosts that haunt this castle are linked to its

terrible past. Back in the days when the castle was a fortress, no one could trust his or her neighbor. Small wars kept the nobility struggling for wealth, land, and power.

One family chieftain sent a goodwill party to Hermitage. He hoped they could make peace with the lord of the castle. Their efforts were wasted, however. The lord of Hermitage put them into a room with no food and water. For food, they tried to eat the flesh from their own arms. Their miserable ghosts are said to haunt the castle ruins.

Another time the ruling lord, Lord de Soulis, invited some nobles to a banquet. The feast was in honor of his daughter's marriage. He had planned to murder the nobles after dinner. Instead he ordered his cook to poison the guests' food. His plan worked so well that they were dead before the last course of the meal.

The most evil lord of Hermitage Castle was Lord de Soulis. He was reputed to be a vicious murderer and black magician. The local people knew he was guilty of terrible deeds. Finally they grew sick of his activities. The lord had killed many members of their families. There are two accounts of how he died.

One story says the people stormed the castle and took him prisoner. Then they tied him with lead bands and boiled him alive in a huge cauldron. Lord de Soulis had been accused of boiling some of his own victims, and this was the way the people took revenge.

In a more realistic account, he was arrested and died in the prison at Dumbarton Castle. Some people think his ghost still haunts the castle. He is said to appear on the anniversary of his death.

Hermitage Castle now stands looking grim and eerie, no longer in use. It waits for any visitor who dares to visit. There is a heavy feeling of warning and danger inside the castle. One famous writer, Sir Walter Scott, had an interesting thought about Hermitage Castle. He said Hermitage Castle sank partly into the ground since it could not hold the burden of wickedness that had taken place within its walls.

Huntingdon Castle

Ireland has many traditions concerning ghosts. It has a large number of castles in historic settings. The Irish people have been telling stories about ghosts for hundreds of years. Of the many haunted castles in Ireland, one is creepy in a friendly way. It is especially nice to ghosts.

The castle is named Huntingdon Castle. It is in County Carlow in Southern Ireland. One must walk through a long walkway of lime trees to reach Huntingdon Castle. It was built in 1625 and, according to the owners, is full of ghosts and strange spirits.

The Durdin-Robertson family has lived in the castle for more than 200 years. One visitor named Simon Marsden, who was interested in haunted places, went to explore Huntingdon Castle. The friendly owners gave him a guided tour.

The castle was full of objects from the past. Marsden saw long, dark corridors. The rooms were full of suits of armor, old tapestries, dusty books, and family portraits. The visitor felt as if he had stepped back in time. The owners had an interesting religion. The Durdin-Robertsons founded a cult called the Fellowship of Isis. Isis was an ancient Egyptian goddess. The fellowship has more than 6,000 members all over the world.

Today, the owners entertain people who claim to be witches. The witches come from different parts of the world. They attend ceremonies that take place in the temple built in the castle dungeons.

The owners are fond of the many ghosts who they say haunt Huntingdon Castle. The family agrees that all ghosts are welcome.

Outside the castle, there is the mysterious 600-year-old Yew Walk, which forms a living tunnel. The ghosts

of the family's ancestors can be seen walking there. In the garden, a ghostly dogcart trots along up the walkway of lime trees.

The ghost of Grace O'Malley, known in legends as the pirate queen, is often seen by the Spy Bush. There she combs her hair by the moonlight.

Inside the castle is a portrait of a woman named Barbara Saint Leger. She came from a famous family of haunts. She married into the Durdin-Robertson family, and now her ghost haunts the chapel. Barbara's maid is also said to be a ghost. She has been seen in the chapel, using her long hair to polish the chapel doors.

There is even a ghostly hand at Huntingdon Castle. One night the owner's daughter felt it while she was asleep in the Yellow Room. A small, cold hand played with her hand and then gave it a tight squeeze.

Sometimes at midnight the ghost of a drunken soldier is heard banging on the door. The owners think he was probably locked out when he was alive in the 17th century.

The ghost of a nurse haunts the castle's Red Room. So does an 18th-century gentleman in a white wig and costume who comes in to investigate the guests who stay there.

The temple in the castle is full of strange relics and statues from many lands. One is the well that the owners say holds magic water. Its contents are used in religious ceremonies.

Huntingdon Castle seems like a friendly haunted castle. The owners are warm and interesting people. Most people are welcome there whether they are living or not.

Calvados Château

Calvados Château was built in 1835 on top of the ruins of an old Norman château. It is located in France. (*Château* is the French word for a feudal castle.) Feudalism was a system in the Middle Ages in which peasants, called vassals, gave their services to the lord of the castle. In exchange, the lord was supposed to protect them.

The history of the ruined feudal château is lost. When the new château was built, people knew only that the area had a reputation for being haunted. Strange noises and tricky ghosts were said to abound in the cold, damp castle.

In 1865, new owners inherited Calvados Château. Almost at once they heard strange noises. No one could find what caused them. It wasn't until ten years later that the ghosts became truly disturbing, however. The owner began to keep a diary, recording all the strange activity in hopes of solving the mystery.

The owner later agreed to let the *Annals of Psychic Science* publish his diary in 1893. He didn't want his name or his family's names to be known. The editor of the *Annals* was impressed with the owner and said, "The honesty and intelligence of the owner of this château cannot be questioned. He himself noted down every day all the extraordinary facts which he and the inhabitants of the château witnessed, just as they occurred."

At first the owner did not believe in ghosts. He was sure someone was trying to scare his family. He thought someone wanted him to move out and sell his haunted château for a low price.

He tried to catch whomever it might be. He secretly put threads across open doors. He searched the whole castle from the cellars to the attic. He tapped on walls looking for long-forgotten passageways or secret rooms. He found nothing.

When there was fresh snow around the castle, he checked for footprints. None were ever found.

Next he bought two large watchdogs. They chased something into a small grove of trees. Soon they came tearing back, terrified, with their tails between their legs. The family searched the woods carefully but did not find anything.

In his diary the owner wrote about strange events in the tutor's room. (The tutor lived at the château to teach the owner's son.)

One night the tutor was alone in his room. At first he heard several raps. Next he heard a large clock winding itself. Then he heard the sound of candlesticks moving across the mantelpiece. By then he was terrified, but he was even more so when he saw his armchair move.

He rang his bedside bell to call for help. When the owner came, he saw that the armchair had moved. He was surprised, since it had been attached to the floor with gummed paper. The candlesticks and a statuette had shifted, too. Later, after the owner had gone back to bed, the tutor heard two heavy blows strike his closet door.

For the next two days, loud noises continued. The noises often sounded like furniture being dragged and dropped with loud thuds.

The owner even heard voices that sounded like their own. There were footsteps and savage hammering sounds on the walls and in rooms upstairs.

The owner would always go and look for the causes himself. He never found anyone or any explanation.

The owner of the château often invited friends and men of the church to his home. They saw and heard the same events and never stayed for long.

Night after night the family heard loud noises. One night everyone was awakened by what sounded like a large bull charging down the stairs. Heavy running noises were heard upstairs.

On another night someone was heard running up the stairs at superhuman speeds. Afterward, the whole château was shaken violently. It was as if a huge log had been flung to the floor. The walls shook nearly to pieces. Four days later, the same thing happened.

On Halloween night the castle was filled with ghostly sounds. The owner wrote that often the footsteps had nothing human sounding about them. He described them as sounding like two legs with no feet.

By November the ghosts had become more violent. Now there were wild screams and long, horrible shrieks. Later in the week, the cries sounded like the cries of demons or the voices of the damned.

Windows and doors opened and closed by themselves. Furniture was tossed around by unseen hands. Beds were turned over and chairs moved from one place to another. The family's Bibles were torn apart.

903466

Then the invisible ghosts began to attack people. At one point the owner's wife reached out to open the door of a room filled with strange noises. Before she could even touch the door, the key turned in the lock. Then it flew out and hit her left hand, bruising it.

Violent hammering on the doors at night sounded like cannonballs being flung. The floors shook with the sounds of stampeding cattle. There were shrieks like the roaring of bulls. Then there was crazy laughter. Everyone heard the same things.

All through the month of January, the family endured the hauntings. The castle would sometimes shake with superhuman blows. At times the blows would come so fast the family could not count them. Still no one was ever seen.

One sunny day the son's tutor was reading in his room. Suddenly a cascade of water gushed down the chimney onto his fire. The ashes and soot covered his room and blinded him briefly.

Three days later everyone heard the voice of a man. Then more sounds shook the castle ten times. In front of the wife's door, they found a broken plate. It had been broken into ten pieces. No one had ever seen the plate in the castle before.

Finally the family grew weary of the trouble. They called a priest to come and get rid of the ghosts. He placed religious objects all around the castle. After the religious rites were performed, everything stopped. Everyone thought the haunting was over. Peace finally came to Calvados Château.

Then one morning the religious objects mysteriously vanished. Several days later they fell from nowhere onto a writing desk where the owner's wife sat.

Months later the noises began again. A couch and some armchairs moved around in a locked room. The organ began playing tunes by itself, even though it had been locked up. The owner kept the key in his pocket and was away on a trip.

After this the hauntings calmed down. The family, however, had had enough of the haunted château. They sold it and moved to a quiet, peaceful place.

By then the owner had recorded more than 100 events in his diary. It is believed that after a second blessing of the castle, the château was finally quiet. No one ever found any clue to what or who had caused the haunting. It is still a mystery. Some ghost hunters say that Calvados Château had one of the most violent poltergeist hauntings in recorded history.

Featherstonhaugh Castle

Featherstonhaugh Castle is in Northumberland, England. It lies in a wooded valley by the banks of the South Tyne River. It is very old and was built in the 12th century. New owners have added rooms to the old castle, so it has gotten bigger over the years, but it still looks like a castle from an ancient fairy tale. It has towers and turrets and ivy-covered walls.

When it was an important stronghold during wars with Scotland, the castle belonged to the powerful Featherstonhaugh family. A legend of a ghostly bridal party is connected to this family. The legend tells a tragic story.

Once there was a powerful and stubborn baron of Featherstonhaugh Castle. He wanted one of his favorite relatives to marry his daughter, Lady Abigail. Abigail did not want to marry her father's choice. She was in love with the son of their sworn enemies, the Ridleys of Hardriding.

She obeyed her father but was sad at the wedding. After the ceremony the members of the bridal party

mounted their horses. They rode out of the castle for a traditional celebration hunt.

The baron and his wife stayed at the castle to oversee the wedding feast. By nightfall the bridal party had not returned. Near midnight the torches and fire were dimming. The servants and entertainers sat in silence. No one dared move. The baron paced up and down in the Great Hall. His wife sat at the table, covering her face with her hands.

Suddenly everyone heard the horses coming across the drawbridge. The huge castle door opened slowly. The bride and groom walked in. The rest of the bridal party were behind them.

To the baron's horror, he saw them walk without a sound right through the furniture. They appeared to be drained of blood. The people in the castle realized they were looking at the spirits of the dead.

When the terrified servants started to run away, a strong wind swept through the Great Hall, and the spirits vanished. The baron went mad from grief that night and never recovered.

After a search, the bodies of the bridal party were found in a nearby glen called Pinkyns Cleugh. It seemed the Ridleys had attacked them and tried to kidnap the bride. Everyone was killed in the attack.

Lady Abigail had tried to stop her husband and the

man she loved from fighting. She had been killed, and then the two men had killed each other.

People still say that, on the anniversary of the day of the battle, the ghostly bridal party can be seen traveling along the road to the gate of Featherstonhaugh Castle.

The Tower of London

The Tower of London is in London, England. It is often called the most haunted place on earth. It was built by William the Conqueror in 1066. He needed a castle to use as a fortress so he could control his new lands. It was the first Norman fortress to be made of stone. To intimidate the city of London, William needed a central fortress that no attacker could burn down.

It was often said that the man who had the tower had the power of the land. For this reason the Tower of London has been the scene of violent struggles for power.

The royal family lived in the tower for 600 years. It

was the safest place for them to stay. The moat was deep. The walls were 15 feet thick at the bottom, 11 feet thick at the top, and 90 feet high.

During King Henry III's reign in the 1200s, the castle walls, both inside and outside, were painted white. Cheerful fires and torches lit up the passageways. Over the years, the floors decayed. The castle became damp and chilly. Without the torches, the passageways looked eerie and the stairways were dark.

From the 11th century on, people plotted to take over the throne. Since the castle was built to keep enemies out, it was also good for keeping prisoners in. New towers and buildings were added to make room for more armies and for prisoners.

High-ranking nobles who were threats to those in power were often accused of treason. These were the kinds of criminals sentenced to the tower.

The tower soon gained a reputation as a place of terror. Being sentenced to the tower was like being given a living death. Many prisoners were tortured there. People could be held in the tower for 15 years before being sentenced. Those sentences were often brutal executions to scare the public and keep them in line.

Methods of execution included beheading with an ax, hanging, or drawing and quartering. Torture was used to get information or confessions and for punishment and revenge.

Later, at Tower Hill, the rulers in power had prisoners executed by burning them on logs. Some had their heads chopped off and put on spikes on the London Bridge. This was to show everyone what would happen to them if they disobeyed.

The rich prisoners could sometimes buy their freedom. It was a good way for the people in power to make money. Wealthy families often had to pay large sums of money to get their captive family members back. Politics could be dangerous and expensive at the tower.

Since so much violence took place at the Tower of London, it is no surprise that hundreds of ghosts have been reported. Some ghost researchers think certain events imprint themselves in the atmosphere at the place where they occurred. They believe people's feelings and emotions leave some kind of energy behind.

This seems true of many of the haunted places in the tower. Famous ghosts are often seen repeating the events of their deaths. Every February 12, the ghost of Lady Jane Grey is said to appear as a white shape near the 13th-century Bloody Tower. That was the date of her execution in 1554.

On May 27, the ghost of Margaret, the countess of Salisbury, is seen reenacting her terrible death. She was innocent but was sentenced to the ax for political reasons. As she was led to the scaffold, she screamed and fought. She challenged the axeman to try to kill her since she was not going to cooperate. She broke free and ran from the scaffold. He chased her, chopping at her with his ax until he killed her.

The ghost of Katherine Howard is often seen running down a haunted gallery. She was one of the wives of King Henry VIII. He was not happy with her and ordered her execution. While she was imprisoned in the tower, she escaped. She ran down the gallery to the Chapel of St. Peter. The king was inside, but he ignored her cries for mercy. She was beheaded, and it is said her ghost still runs down the gallery begging for mercy.

Henry VIII had his second wife, Anne Boleyn, beheaded in 1536. She had the public's sympathy. Her ghost has been seen by many people who recognize her from her portrait.

One guard saw her ghost in 1864, more than 300 years after her death. He was at his post and saw a woman who was all white move toward him. He charged at her with his pikestaff, which went right through her. He was so frightened he fainted.

The authorities charged him with not staying on duty. They thought he had fallen asleep. While he was on trial, Major Dundas came forward and said that he had been looking out of the tower window and saw the event happen. The place had a reputation for being haunted, so the charges were dropped.

A lot of famous ghosts seem to haunt different parts

of the tower. The ghosts of two small boys are said to haunt the Bloody Tower, which was earlier known as the Garden Tower. The two boys were princes, the sons of King Edward V. When the princes were only 12 and 9 years old, their uncle Richard, the duke of Gloucester, took them away from their mother. He put them in the Bloody Tower, and they were never seen again. Since the country needed a king, the duke inherited the title. It is thought that King Richard III had murdered his nephews so he could have the throne.

In 1674, two small skeletons were discovered in a chest beneath the stairway of the White Tower. It is a good guess that the skeletons belonged to the two missing princes. Their sad little ghosts have been seen walking hand in hand in the Bloody Tower.

The White Tower is part of the original Norman castle. The royal family lived in the White Tower with all the fortress's protection. There is a well in the basement for water.

The Great Council Chamber was here. Some great decisions of history, such as when to go to war, were made here. Down below was a dungeon with a torture chamber. Kings and queens, lords and ladies, servants and soldiers — all lost their lives in the White Tower.

Tales of evil and suffering and the cries of victims in the dungeon seem to echo through the centuries. People have reported noises and sounds of screams. There

were cold drafts when all the windows were tightly shut. Some people have even smelled incense as if from a time long ago. Even the experienced castle guards agree the White Tower is no place to be at night.

There are so many ghosts in other towers, it is difficult to record them all. The ghost of King Henry VI, who was stabbed to death, is often seen at Wakefield Tower between 11 P.M. and midnight.

Saint Thomas's Tower is named after Thomas à Becket. He was the archbishop of Canterbury. This tower is cursed. Doors are said to open and close by themselves. A ghostly monk dressed in brown moves around in the tower shadows.

Tower Green is a garden where the king had a private scaffold for personal use. The ghost of Anne Boleyn has been seen here, and often she is headless.

Beauchamp Tower is one of the more popular towers for prisoners of noble birth. A well-dressed ghost has been seen here by a tower guide.

The famous explorer Sir Walter Raleigh was the victim of political trouble. His mischievous ghost is said to haunt the Bloody Tower, where he was kept as a prisoner for 13 years. He was executed in 1618.

During the day, the Middle Tower is haunted by the sound of footsteps pacing the battlements. Sentries guarding the entrance to this tower have been shocked by the sight of ghostly troops of soldiers marching on grim missions. Phantoms of knights and their ladies have been seen in the Chapel Royal of Saint Peter ad Vinculas, on the castle grounds. The ghostly procession is led by a spirit who looked like Anne Boleyn. Her body lies buried beneath an altar there.

Several ghosts have been reported in the Martin Tower, and just a few yards from the Salt Tower, workmen discovered a skeleton 15 feet down. The grave contained a young man from 2,000 years ago. His skull had a hole in it, and his knees were bent to show a violent death. Who he was or why he was killed is a mystery, but one of the ghosts near the tower could belong to him.

The past seems to reach out with its ghosts and spirits. They remind us of the violence and horror that took place in historic castles. Perhaps only those who are sensitive to the past can see them. If you have a chance to visit a creepy castle, you might see one, too.

For Further Reading

Abbott, G. *Ghosts of the Tower of London.* Portsmouth, N.H.: Heinemann Educational Books, Inc., 1980.

Cohen, Daniel. *The Encyclopedia of Ghosts.* New York: Dodd, Mead & Co., 1984.

Deem, James M. *How to Find a Ghost.* Boston: Houghton Mifflin Co., 1988.

Holzer, Hans. *Hans Holzer's Haunted Houses.* New York: Crown Publishers, Inc., 1971.

Kettelkamp, Larry. *Haunted Houses.* New York: William Morrow & Co., 1969.

— *Mischievous Ghosts: The Poltergeist and PK.* New York: William Morrow & Co., 1980.

Knight, David C. *The Moving Coffins: Ghosts and Hauntings Around the World.* New York: Prentice-Hall, Inc., 1983.

Osborne, Will. *13 Ghosts: Strange But True Stories.* New York: Scholastic Inc., 1980.

Simon, Seymour. *Ghosts.* Philadelphia, Pa.: J. B. Lippincott Company, 1976.

Underwood, Peter. *The Ghost Hunter's Guide.* New York: Blanford Press, 1986.

Index